LOOSE TO THE WORLD

OTHER BOOKS BY
HENRY RAPPAPORT

Heat in the Heart

Are Words Things?

A Book of Days

Dream Surgeon

loose
TO THE
world

– poems –

for Gillian

HENRY RAPPAPORT

RONSDALE

LOOSE TO THE WORLD
Copyright © 2014 Henry Rappaport

RONSDALE PRESS
3350 West 21st Avenue
Vancouver, B.C., Canada V6S 1G7
www.ronsdalepress.com

Typesetting: Julie Cochrane, in New Baskerville 11 pt on 13.5
Cover Design: Julie Cochrane
Cover Art: "Strong Roots" by Jo Rappaport
Paper: Enviro 100 Edition, 55 lb. Antique Cream (FSC) — 100%
    post-consumer waste, totally chlorine-free and acid-free

Ronsdale Press wishes to thank the following for their support of its publishing program: the Canada Council for the Arts, the Government of Canada through the Canada Book Fund, the British Columbia Arts Council, and the Province of British Columbia through the Book Publishing Tax Credit Program.

Library and Archives Canada Cataloguing in Publication

Rappaport, Henry, 1944–, author
  Loose to the world: poems / Henry Rappaport.

Issued in print and electronic formats.
ISBN 978-1-55380-338-6 (print)
ISBN 978-1-55380-339-3 (ebook) / ISBN 978-1-55380-340-9 (pdf)

  I. Title.

PS8585.A66L66 2014   C811'.54   C2014-901459-7   C2014-901460-0

Printed in Canada by Marquis Book Printing, Quebec, Canada

for Jo, Ben and Mark

ACKNOWLEDGEMENTS

Grateful acknowledgement is made to the following publications in which these poems first appeared, sometimes in previous versions:

"Spilled Milk" in *American Poetry Journal*; "Happy Endings" in *Interim*; "Sense of Place" in *Forge*; "Poet Seeks Cabin with View" in *Schuykill Valley Journal of the Arts*; "Tomorrow" *in Ken Again*; "To . . ." in *The Broome Review*; "Signs of the Season" and "The Casualties of Where" in *The Café Review*; "Getting Along" in *Ship of Fools*; "After the Fall" in *Quiddity*; "Morning" in *The Cincinnati Review*; "Table Talk" in *Poet Lore*; "After Dinner at the Foothills Café" in *The Cape Rock*; "What the Poem is About" in *Squaw Valley Review*; "How Come?" in *Fifth Wednesday Journal*; "There Ain't Nothing" in *Rocksalt*; "Fruit" in *Argestes*; "The Rialto" in *Juked*; "After the Storm" in *Grain*; "Walking Her Home" in *West Coast Review*; "Peggy" in *Westview*.

Thanks to the following poets for their guidance: Jen Currin, Karen Solie, Betsy Warland, Jami Macarty, Robert Hass, Cornelius Eady, Claudia Emerson, James Longenbach, Mary Szybist, Eavan Boland and Don McKay. Thanks also to Sage Hill, Squaw Valley, Sewanee, Bread Loaf, Tin House and Napa for the opportunity to write in a community, and thanks to those communities. And to the memories of Robert Allen Durr and Donald Justice.

CONTENTS

~ I ~

– III –

– Afterword –

Lucid his project lay, beyond. Can he?
Loose to the world lay unimaginable Henry,
loose to the world,
taut with his vision as it has to be,
open & closed sings on his mystery
furled & unfurled.

— JOHN BERRYMAN

–I–

There Ain't Nothing

for Karen Solie

Aretha sings *there ain't nothing like the real thing*
and I agree. Someone overhears and says,
nothing profound in that, and I agree with that too.

A picture on a wall, for instance,
will not answer when Aretha calls its name;
it cannot move her or groove her like the sound
of his sweet voice whispering in her ear.
It cannot hold her like the hold of his strong arms.

When he was an infant
I held Benjamin in my arms, and
we danced in the living room of her song,

the man and the picture of that man, the song
and the singer of that song, its writer, those words,
that infant in my arms.

His Name Was Ken

My mother-in-law looks at the world through a small window
she would like to have cleaned but she can't get it done.
So I come over to take her out for coffee,
and as her wheelchair bumps over the careful violence
of the street, she says be careful not to spill me out.
I am very careful especially when we go downhill
and I have to lean back so she doesn't roll away
and pour out in front of the coffee shop.

She doesn't want to wear the yellow sunglasses
we bought her at the institute, but when we get outside
I can tell the glare is too much for her, so I lean over
and put mine on her and it's better.
She wonders if we're lost, and I say no
we just haven't been here before
so it's a new experience like landing on the moon,

and she remembers watching that on TV with me
while her daughter was at a rehearsal
where the director wouldn't let them stop
and I say no that wasn't me.
I don't know where I was at the time,
but it wasn't there.

She likes her sweets but worries about gaining weight
and I say hey! go for it — at ninety-one what have you got
to lose? And she tells me about her sister who died
and left some money to her grandson
who called to say it wasn't enough
and she becomes livid and sad.

I bring her the smallest latte they have so it won't keep her up.
She looks at her watch, and I tell her not to worry
I'll be sure to have her back in time for supper. After all, I say,
it's not like returning from the moon.
It's not like that movie
where they almost didn't make it back.

She's been to the moon too many times
and it's just too boring, she says.
She doesn't want to go again.
And then she asks if I remember the time
and I say no, that was another time.
His name was Ken.

I take her back a smoother way.
As I wheel her into the hall, we hear a thwack
and she says tennis. Then I take her
into her room and she thanks me
as she settles in to watch the world on TV.

My Book of Words

Each day I make this world
one word at a time
bathroom   sink   the critical
comb that mocks my hair,
Mr. Mirror
who mimics my face
my teeth my
indentured smile.

This world of my imagining —
is it any wonder I get it muddled
and confused?
Each day like leaves
the words fall away
and a tree remains
that ramifies
into empty air.

Such is my paradise —
the lifeless load
I do not lift
the splash
of waking
the fresh
face there.

Music on Lincoln Road

I'd like to play for you
by ear, jam if I can.
The lessons I learned
were so canned
with the metronome
always on tock
tic tock tic tock.

When my tune
takes a wander
I sometimes
know where to put
a foot down
on the shovel
that digs
the song I sing.

I'm happy to spend
happy times with you
when the blues riff
away
happy to sing
in the improvised sun
songs for supper
and for fun.

In Disarray

I staggered early into disarray.
I slept in fields of every thought
where I stood brazen with beliefs.
I thought all thinkers drank the dawn.

I sang the praise of every day
from sight's momentum
on dew wet on grass
to legends I learned by feel.

And then I read the holy
texts of this and that.
I have to admit I could
not believe in any of it.

How could I live in consequence
who lived so long in disarray?

Bonneville

A car drives into the ambiguous light
of September when they go to Syracuse
where fall hides like a meaning in a book.
It is a borrowed, temporary light as many know
who have studied there. At the end of their
exhausting journey along a two-lane road that used
to be the only way they are relieved to have arrived.

Three of them drive the leather seats, turquoise trim
and stereo speakers front and rear after Labour Day
when the busy tourist season is done. It is still warm
enough to keep the top down. The three of them
pass through farm country and small towns
until they reach the dorm where they let him off.
Out of the trunk of the white car he takes
the black foot locker he will live from for the rest
of his life. She stays with her friend in a nearby motel.
The next morning after goodbyes the two women drive home.

By bus or by thumb or with a ride from a friend
over the next five years he takes Route-17 home
and back to university again. There is no other way.
The farms are empty, the animals are gone
except for a few black birds that fly into the leafless fields.
Once into the dark around Binghamton he hitches
to the bypass and walks to his home almost too late
to find her in bed with the *Daily News*. They ask
each other how they are.
                            Then she sells and
moves to a small motel. The once he visits
he plays "Sgt. Pepper's" and sleeps on the floor.

Winter Works

Through the leafless trees
the deer tongues
freeze in the snow.

Their melting
blood
brings spring.

The Rialto

About friends
I learned from a
chimpanzee,
about love from a crash
into a dark place.

To leap I learned
from a man who
threw himself
singing from vine
to vine.

I ate with fingers
and let peels
fall where they
might.

Names I learned by
candlelight
as chimps came to call
laughing
I could talk
their talk.

Gibberish to some —

a man, a boy,
a woman
living
in a tree.

The Poem

As in an eye, as eye,
seeing
as from the centre of a storm
you wear in your eye,
everyone wears.

As in song, as if song, as song.
Senseless and the same.
An old dirt road
that is where it wants to go.
Your way home.

Jack

Jack was simple some will say.
Others too quick to run away.

Jack took my boots and warmed my feet
when I came through ice and sleet.

Jack took my coat and warmed my heart.
Always with outsides Jack would start.

Jack saw what no one else would see,
he took the baggage and he took me.

Jack built me a sometime home
I thought he was building from stone.

Jack took me to where I was born
and left me torn.

Waiting for Papa

The ferry rocks toward a suburb
with nice determination. Piano-tutored
children walk dogs among the dahlias,
over rocks, across paths long and
gaping as an elephant's trunk.

A nice woman, once indeterminately
beautiful, polishes her piano, ferries
the straps of her dreams to the edge
of the suburb, waits, remembers the dahlias,
waits for her husband, a rock of a man.

How the Circle Was Squared

Gail takes me to her place
to spend the night.
She sleeps us,
her daughter, Linda, and me,
touch to touch.
In the morning
we fold the couch
and push it out of the way.
Gail says she is going to
teach us to something.
The music she puts on
is soft and low.
It's no rock and roll.
Around and around
in our arms we go
each step a corner
each corner a step.
Oh, I don't know,
maybe eight or nine.
How could I know
what this love is?

Estelle

I see her work the scrub
that stains her knees
and mints her hands
under the old cedar
where she hopes
to grow flowers.

I see her make up
at her table of half-full bottles
and nameless jars.

I see her hurry
to run a shift at Jack's
where she can
live up
to her name.

Vietato Fumare

Of course you could make a scene
with a man and a woman
a cigarette burning down
its long ash in an ashtray
when people smoked. You could
say the affair ends as he watches
the ash lengthen listening to her
crying while he waits for her
to grasp the situation
and compose herself.

He could say *look, things end,*
time passes, nothing lasts.
He might flick it,
take a last drag and exhale
then stub it out. Or he might sit
and watch as it consumes itself.

Things are different now.
The scenes snappier.
The symbols not so obvious.
We know smoke kills.
And who says she would be
the one crying?

The Bridge

I raced my father to the bridge and won
then stood winded in the darkness waiting for him.

He laughed at my running so hard
as if there were something to win.

There was something important he wanted to say,
and then I turned and he was gone.

Burning Leaves

Sometimes in autumn
among deciduous trees
I stand and say goodbye
to my dead poems.

Then, in the here
and now
of my expired
expectations

I feel the rush
of leaves
raked into flames
that say what they see.

Against a sky full of smoke
I inhale and admire
how a single leaf holds on
like something I keep trying to say.

The Bluff

In a past away from me
a fire had stained
a ring of stones
where I first walked
into the woods
behind our house
to pick blueberries.
If I touch those rocks
my fingers come back
black.

At play on a pile
of dirt on the other side
of Starr Avenue,
I was called to lunch.
I sat at the table, I ate.
I was almost run over
trying to return.

Today

In the morning
we say
today

and at night
we say
this way to the light.

Yesterday
we said tomorrow,
and tomorrow we will say yesterday.

Much to Admire

Before I woke this morning, I was naïve.
My weight the same, and no pest came
to eat the broccoli I forgot on the stove.

I slept again. I dreamed the suicide
from the night before was not mine.
Nothing needed to be done.

In my own time I could figure out why
or not. I went back to sleep, and awoke again,
opened the mail and read the news.

I became confused. The light of pure reason
dimmed. I only got what I wanted
and what never was became never again.

– II –

Getting Up

Before sleep, I cleared out.
But this morning you came
in the shape of a girl
I almost made it with,
a girl so late last night
I forgot to cast her
up and out
of the centre of my head
where she lay sleeping,
dreaming of being
the only thought I had
to awaken to.
I didn't see
even her face
among the beasts
snorting through the jungle
below my window.
When a man shifts gears
I know it
no matter when
or where he's going.
I know his style
and the kind
of love he makes
by whether he wakes me.

Asking Ganesh

I want to ask Ganesh
to sit with me at the window
and help me perceive
significance.

Call it itch of doubt
about seeking
more
metaphor.

Should I swan
the I, spin yin
and yang
until it all goes grey?

I want to say
I hope his trip
in my suitcase
was ok.

I hope he likes it
on the walnut
table
in our hall.

I wonder does he
miss the incense
of appetite and the colour
of sensual days.

I do Zazen.
I do Tai Chi.
I bust my ass in Core.
He knows what for.

Sanches Pasquas

I go to hear pretty teeth
speak green vegetables

to see the keen blade
unquiver the thighs

that yesterday pissed the field.
I go to tamales

to husk and tell,
to see the old man's eyes

take emptiness from my hands
with a wooden spoon.

After the Storm

Rain slicked the pavers' thick thirst
with last night's trash and fallen leaves
as a woman dancing unclothed
in front of a man leaning on a broom.

In late fields, birds ate what remained
on bare trees, and into windfalls
soft ground animals ate holes.
The woolly apple drank and fell
where the mouth that bit went dry.

Hard softened into pale
where fall sustained the few remaining
rosehips boys used to bite for pips
they put down people's backs
to make them itch.

The air was single and still
except for a bird calling
and a sweeper standing amazed
at the unclothed beauty dancing
before his eyes.

Signs of the Season

1

Rosie says
the bush is December
thinks three weeks freeze got it
is flip and sad at the half masts.

Meanwhile, the sun knocks its head
on the year's first bee.

What am I sure of?

That everything I want
is on the table
in the empty glass?

2

The man is sad
who writes about sadness
whose graveyard
is the woman he loved
who hung November from a tree
discovered
March
in his heart.

He felt like true dirt
packed a bag
and found a white cat
to nap on his lap.

3

One good Friday,
John Donne and I
dragged our asses out of April
to the library in downtown Syracuse.
He felt half giddy and half sad and turned around.
He asked that he be present yet
unto my memory.

Now every spring he blows it
and I remember
Syracuse.

4

Is the world
friend
to circumstance
does it smile
as it sees
through a window
into itself ?
and does it
adore sleep
when sleep comes
to the mortal country?

5

I listened to the woman on TV
say *I'll be right back.*
I waited until I heard her sing

nothing

lasts forever

not a glass

full of

emptiness

not

a

sugarless

bush

into which

sugars

flow.

Tomorrow

Tomorrow thinks
when its time comes
it will be
more like today.

It skims the paper
that hit the door at 3 a.m.
so it can plan what to do
to keep its promise
to be ahistorical.

Meanwhile today
soaks into the bushes
under the eaves
and looks at the dark
from which it also comes.

It knows it is not tomorrow
nor ever will be.

Fruit

She meets him in the early
evening after the trees are

picked clean, walks beside him
as the sun flashes late light

through the filtering leaves.
All day he tallied and weighed

abundance
until she arrived.

Then what difference season
or light or count or time to them?

Poet Seeks Cabin with View

A couple of gulls from the right rock
did a chimney sweep after a faint call,
and the only word the water made
was from being turned by the prop
of an early pleasure, the sound of soup.
The scarf of seaweed on the beached log
was less itself than the day before
dissolving and drying like linen on a line.
The sun addressed questions of the day
no one was asking tucked
into long folds of their slow waking.
Light on the necks of the sea followed
in the immature day as shadow followed
thing as a young gull follows older.
Then the air moved to chill, a gang
of clouds came from around the corner
and a car spun stones in the parking lot.
The morning filled with emptiness:
was the slow craft trolling, where was the car
going, would clouds stutter the sun?
Then conversations began between body
and bed, foot and floor, bacon and air.

Spilled Milk

Flowers appeared
and then a frost
disappeared them
and sad was in season.
Next time February comes
with pretend on its face
we will know better.

I sometimes wonder who
else is living in this body —
the one who knocks things over.
As with flowers above,
I've come to expect mis-
steps, but it's nothing
to spill about.
When I see the mug
upended in tears,
I wonder who is that?

At Zumba I rarely fail.
To the music
I make my moves
and once in a while
the song seems profound.
*No soy de aquí, no soy
de allá* she sings.

That's how I feel.

No soy de aquí, no soy de allá: I am not from here; I am not from there

Make Dead

Make dead the light
and lie with me
to touch and hear
in the dark song
how longing
sweetens sleep.

Touch the dark shore
I am for you.
In the morning
like the light,
for me, make
dead the night.

Walking Her Home

I don't think she knew
that first night
if what she felt was right.
I could sort of tell
from how she held her hands
that she was afraid.
It was dark
and the storm had littered
the beach with logs.
A shipwreck scattered
rusty fangs
and hid them well
over a mile in the sand.
I offered to walk her home.

At first we went over loose sand
slowly, high stepping,
then faster below the tide line
talking about walking.
The night was clear
not bright
and each star studied its sky.
A night only fear or evil could enhance.
A year alone with a sick man
held more by sickness than her love
taught her to fear everything —
night in the trees, old whispers,
this beach she'd walked a hundred times before.

Her home was sheet plastic
and thin cedar framing
and was set away in the logs.
Too low to stand in,
to narrow to make love,
it was a proper nun's cell
or monk's as she said.
And it was in the darkest spot
with no chance of light from the sea
or from campfires up the beach.
She had come to be alone
and the loneliest place picked her.
I doubt if ever during the day
even the sun, bare chested,
could have reached her.

On her stoop I sat and talked
about old intellectual things,
Soul's unanimity, the one Body
in the one Mind, good books.
With grace she placed her right foot
gently against her other thigh
and kept her back straight
a ballerina's pose.
The candle she lit was low
so I decided to go
and said goodnight.

I tumbled over her fence
back to the sand
and walked toward the high meadow
set on a massive rock
at the edge of the ocean.
The wind cackled like leaves
fall lets hang in the trees.

I looked up the long backlit grasses
and felt something I cannot explain.
Something there or in me
from where I'd been
pierced night right through me
and tore me like a tarp
flapping in the wind.

I didn't climb onto the jut of stone
where I'd put a hole in the sky
but turned directly home.
She came down the next day
said my monument blew down
and sort of stayed.
Within a week she moved our way for good.

The Odds of a Good Night's Sleep

Eight on the toes of five
six of two
midnight of three
a spit from quarter to
to just this side of another half
a strip of beaded water
from a breath in a room of titles
squeezed shoulder to shoulder
weighed down under the wisdom of a word
     mirror   mirror   mirror
tricking the quick second
in the feeble radiated dark
of any a.m. ask who should know
seven closer to four
the barefoot tiptoe
peek up the skirt
of the hopeful light
six forty-nine nine to three
seven to eleven ten to one.

The Clearing

The long sought for
comes directly at you
through an inlet you noticed
and studied and drew
but never saw before.
Now it draws you
out of yourself
and into the perpetual
beginning and ending of things.
This is not the first time
nor will it be the last.
Joy swells within and you sing
songs sweet enough for any air.
Here, here, you sing, and now.
Between me and what I see
lives eternity.

What Did You Do?

I did not walk on still water
in the seaside pool
or in the afternoon calm
after the big blow.

I did not warm myself at the campfire
of *kum-by-ya* or dip my finger into the cocoa
of goodnight. Although I heard them,
I did not go.

I did not play card games,
word games, guessing
games of chance or puzzle
pieces into the picture of anything.

I did not paddle, boat, bike, soak,
serve or return, swim through the scum,
source wood for a stove, make field trips,
or search a book for the name of anything at all.

I did not rush to the rescue of the kayaker
flipped by the storm. I did not sit patiently
waiting for the idiot sun to keep its promise.
I did not have a bad time.

On Reading Ruth Stone's
"What We Have" for Dessert

So we're talking about how
some wars are malevolent
but all are testosterone-induced
and the women mostly agree
except for a reference to the Amazons.

Aren't they all malevolent
someone asks,
and the one who proposed it
says *no*, some are for
protection of a way of life
defence agains pillage, plunder
and rape. Once the fighting begins
it's all outrage and revenge.

Trying to recall where it went from there,
lunch on a beach in Mykonos,
cloth umbrellas, nothing too heavy
like butchered lamb.

Or maybe Kindle vs. iPad,
a civilized skirmish
we could agree not to agree on.
A lot of our choices, it's pointed out,
aren't e-anywhere, e-anyway.

During the lull, I wonder
why not benevolence for dessert?
I find the poem and read it from my phone.

I Ask a Friend
to Find My Brother's Grave

for Barry Schacht

It doesn't matter
which way
he lies.

There is no
telling him
to turn.

Or if the sun
is over his left
or north shoulder

but in which row
and where exactly
if you can.

And the headstone.
Tell me,
what does it say?

Not

   spring falling down the white
mountain, not the climb up a green trail

beyond what we can see. Not the orange
hoarding blocking the street-end view.

Not the yellow raincoat in its hurry
to university. Not the rip saws of new construction,

not the hammer nor the claw or the continuous
emptying into the public drain flushing for fall. Not

branches standing in a vase
with fists unclenched to scent the living room.

Not the seasonal sweep, not the hidden goodbye
to the draped window whose light nevertheless

floods the floor. Not pleasant peasant dreams
with some unhappy harvests. Not the storms,

not winter's dumplings, not the heat turned down,
not the pj's, not the extra blanket, not the crack and blow

of arctic air, not the wool socks from Connemara shrunk to fit.
Not destination. Not the pen holding the hand as if it had
                              something to say.

Driving Home on the Day of the Dead

for B. M. Spaethe

When the clocks crank back and we awake,
figures swim into plain sight and exhaust
themselves from grin to silly grin.

The fruit ripening in the large white bowl,
the painted toy, the cushion pricked with pins
say *Red. Stop Here!*

As the dying picnic on mounds of their
dead, black-hatted broom-riders open
their cloaks and fly like bats out of hell

close enough to reveal their names
Sun Stalker, Seeker of the Cold Light,
Clock Tosser.

Then the dark joy drives into the momentous
stuff of life and the world remembered
hurts itself into song.

To

        prune limbs though why
eagerness should be called
leggy is hard to say, to feed
compost worms, to suppose
harvest from quiet things
that percuss when they shake
like castanets, to do diligence
due the earth, to clean, to carry,
to trash, to free light from its bed,
to de-leaf the fountain, to fill
the birdbath, to shape diminishing
since that's what pruning is
but that's not all of it, to add to,
to be in the act of, to ponder,
to say
        yellow, say pink.

Pender Harbour

for Barb Nield

Above an old foreshore lease, a framed map hangs
from a hundred years ago. On it highways criss-
cross the sea and easements scale unscalable cliffs.
Names that were nailed down and staked to places
get worked up in the slack and swell of season
like a rusty spike on the dock where you can get hurt
if you don't watch out. When who knows where
we are and if we want to weather right
we need a map that changes as we change.

South of Agamemnon, between Williams and Charles
almost blinded by Pearson and Martin, Nares
like a finger points to the phantom dock of the first village
where left to dawn and right to twilight winds riff
the wet back-mix of black water into a playground
as long as it's breezy and light. How do you get there?
Not from sleep above bi-valves, but after a long parch
by being pulled to John Henry's to drink and scan
a ceiling patching eighty-year old chart. And then
by clawing past the muck and rasp of thick and
low to slap over fresh mottle into meandering.

On a say-so you get there. Milky morning light
an old boat with three drunk Scotsmen
dancing in the bow, loose-lips in the rigging,
dissipated pontoons, the choral suck
& fresh jetsam the ear twitches to.

After the Fall

The lion asks the arrow
to stay away from its life,
asks the bow to live alone
to stay part of the tree.

Villagers ask the lion to be a rug,
to snore for them as they sleep,
to protect them
with its confident heart.

Hunters in hiding ask to see
the tethered neck
snapped
not consumed.

They with their guns ask for fun
a sensual thing.
When they are done
they will love again.

Black Bird

I saw the great wings open.
Why should I fear?
It flew away.
I wrote and read.
The day was fair.
The bird was black.
The pen was midnight blue.

How Come?

That's what happens
when you think it's in the bag,
when you fall off the wagon, go over
a cliff, asleep at the wheel, when you don't
pull over, don't pull your weight, take your eye
off the ball in this neck of the woods.
That's what happens when you build it,
they come and the bleachers fail,
when you think you're a stand-up, shoulder-
to-shoulder, eye-to-eye guy. That's what happens
when you shoot your wad, play dead,
go belly up, a big fish in a small pond.
Let me tell you before it's too late,
that's what happens when you open
your big mouth, stray, welsh, turn a deaf ear,
a blind eye, lean on children, feed weeds,
connive, deal in false deeds, drift, marry
wrong, snitch, keep turning over a new leaf,
bitch about the cat you let out of the bag
after you spilled the milk. Listen.
Before it's too late. Your heart
is wearing out on your sleeve.
That's what happens.

Light Talk

When they meet by chance in the lane
she says from her van, *You've ruined
it for me*, and he says *I'm glad
I can do something right.*

And her smile behind the wheel
does not diminish one bit.
She wants to tell him
he is getting on.

Street and house lights
had just begun to glimmer
through the full darkness
that covered the lane

behind her new house —
a little less beautiful,
needing a little more care now
he had dubbed it the *Chateau.*

A car coughed in the early distance
and reflections from the north shore
began to signal as branches swayed
in and out of the way.

Quiet and still, they took their time
in the diminishing dark before they
remembered their must-do's
must-not says and she drove away.

Gliding

If I were an airplane
I would be swift
if ash
I would float on moods of air
empty of joy
of care.

After Dinner at the Foothills Café

In the strip mall
at the foot of the foothills
a man walks out of the dark
café into a boozy light
from the fluorescent
laundromat next door.

In the residual heat of day
he eases out of his coat
and two-steps
a pair of boots
to the edge of the lot
where a metal fence
stands beside the river.

It never floods
even in spring
in this valley
of dry grasses
and wine.

He kicks a stone or two
to ping a can
and gentles his boot
under a rung
as he leans on the rail
and the river
which also has had its fill
chews on a long
blade of grass.

He looks up and whistles
and makes a wish
as he moves
a toothpick
across his mouth.
Or does the stick stay still
as his head
moves
side to side.

The Casualties of Where

for Jen Currin and Jami Macarty

A man in the night
looks at a map.
He looks and wonders
where he can go.

He closes his eyes
tired of looking
at a map for a place
he cannot see.

He sits in a chair
and thinks
his nowhere
is everywhere.

Sunday's Poem

for Robert Hass

The man who has
seeks his hunger
wherever he goes.

The man without
opens his hands
to a song in the trees.

How can the man
with nothing
give his hunger
to the man who is full?

Skookumchuck

for John Nield

Not on water
would you come
to this place
nor at any time
except perhaps
when slack

separates early
from early
and late from late
and always
to see the radar-
poised shark-
confident mouth
chew things.

Best by land
through division
and subdivision
to observe
as a personal thing
the deep decline
so as to return
abundant
sleek and slow
muscular
in the tide-scrubbed
wash-light
to tug keen
in the confident spin,

sail-less, putt putt by putt,
rain-spat, diminutive,
sun-bit but nimble
still, swift or slow
                              into the swirl
                    putt putt
by putt
at self speed
unlocked
from the landlocked way.

Past commerce
past sphagnum packed
fractures
past elbows and femurs
of cedar and fir —
past the moss-gloved markers
and latticed restraints
to see the relentless
roil and fall.

Table Talk

The salt asks
whose fault is it
I am not a mountain

and the red wine
replies
you do what you can.

The fork, the knife
and the spoon say
open wide

and the virgin
napkin pressed
against red lips
asks
what have I done?

– III –

Object Lessons

for the Qu'Appelle

The side of the valley I study every day,
the tidy farm, the barn the cows return to,
the round metal roof, the mounds
that protect it, not eskers or moraines,
the green of spring not climbing yet
out of the trees, close to horizon
where east comes from.

Two lanes running downhill from Regina
to Saskatoon and two back, a van moving
with a houseful, a semi full of packaged goods
for stores to sell, a two-bed tanker of Co-Op gas.
Since I can't see inside, it's all a guess.
Decide to drive that road, sometime.

Two robins close enough to see
hop across the lawn. Eat ticks do they?
Hope so. Snow gone from the ridge
its back to the sun. Outbuilding on a pile of dirt
in the centre of a lawn, windowless, wireless,
a black pipe to vent.
                    Another weathered away
mineralizing the flats near the railroad track.
That's memory. And trees opening, that's time
and promise. Isn't it?

Kettle on a roll rumbles and boils
to the odd spoon clank, pan, voice, pot,
whistles minimalist music
through the open refectory door
into the tidy room where we will sit.
Can we really be hungry
again? That's the imperative
right now. Present tense.

Thing Is

It said turn the handle
wait five minutes
then fill it to the line.

Shake the thing and plug it in.

Don't do this in the bathroom, it said.
Kitchen is best.

Switch it on and wait
five minutes or more
while it does its thing.

Then turn it off and let it stand
a week or so.

Place it in the fridge
if you have the space.

Then repack
thing and contents
into the original box
right side up
and put it at the curb
on garbage day.

Bull Vonse

Yesterday was my birthday
and my family dearly departed
showed up to share their best wishes.
My mother had a fifties perm
and her swooped pink glasses edged up.
My father drove his Lincoln
and when he saw my crew cut
he said *Polak, Happy Birthday, Polak,*
as on the day he died.

They were just like the neighbors when I was a kid
who packed their car to go on holiday,
opened their windows, smiled their smiles,
and turned to wave from the back seat
to say goodbye and to let me know
there was no happiness like theirs.
And when I got used to no one
to play with, to the comfort of their absence
they turned up, fed up with fun.

Yesterday my wobbly family returned
to bend and chastise the upright,
to offend and shake the grace of the young
and my grandmother called me a *bull vonse.*
I'm still not exactly sure what that means
but I knew it wasn't *Happy Birthday.*

The living came too. As I seeded my garden
they channeled signals from outer space
and sang me a proper birthday song —
something like live and be well
in your original skin.

Yesterday turned out better than ok.
Although it had pissed like endless crying
the blues faded and there were no more tears.
The dead schlepped their dreadful baggage away
for good. And we had *kir royale,*
barbecued ribs and Dairy Queen.

Tea

The Silk Road organic serenity on the counter in its tin.
In what sense is it what it says it is? Or for that matter
how does my watching make chores grow
like grass on the lawn I mowed yesterday,
clipped and even and nothing left?

In the back-yard sunlight, a swarm of bugs
jives Saturday night at the Crystal Palace
to no purpose I can see, not like the bee
soft shoeing its two step all over the sex
organs of the lavender, flagrant,
fragrant without much say.

Most of the vegetables are still sleeping
after their drench in the irrigated dark.
A single leaf dies in pirouettes and then
the stiff bow of movement completed
without sound and a chore is born.
By its leaving an early jet defines east
and silence like the intimate humming
of the hummingbird I turn to see flit away.

On the dead branch of our old mac, a clematis finds
a crutch. That's why we won't cut it, that and the
feng shui wabe sabi of the old tree. Every year we prune
suckers and headers and the runt and rotten windfalls
I take to the compost bin. It's work I like.

The sun this morning actually insists on shorts,
so I disrobe into almost entirely only me.
To the buzzing beside my ear I don't have to explain
it's not an orifice of engendering.
To the fly on the back of my hand
I don't have to say it tickles
as it probes for a rotten spot to lay its eggs
that will hatch into maggots — not yet.

That impulse to shoo and swat is absent
as if there were nothing not to love out here.
Not the rough rock wall I built with inexperience
straining to put the heavy stones on top
where they were sure to fall. Not the yellow jacket
that drinks curiosity at the sweet black lip of my coffee mug
(four times I have been stung upsetting their nest
in the compost bin). Not the odd airbeater
or the persistent jets that make waves in the sky.
Not the irregular falling up and down hill to UBC.

When I heard squeals that sounded like the joy of a bug
in pollen, the stiff glee of a gate opening, fabric
easing into the shape of my own shape on a sometime
chair, for no reason fathomable by me,
all these things were the furthest thing from bother,
like the gift of a tea of serenity someone gave us
a long time ago that had gone unmissed and forgotten,
out of sight on the bottom of a much-used drawer.

My Plan

I arrange this life
as well as I can.

I try not to care
if I care.

The facts
are all there

no one sins
to be saved.

I do what I can
to be as I am

wherever I can
whenever I am.

Peggy

for Peggy Nolan

In short-sleeve October
both of us away from home
we used to walk the Ave.
and talk in the bright sunlight
that spiked off stands whose news
we never read. I kept trying to tell her
how I always felt lonely with her.
I don't think she knew.
On those early, empty streets
she would talk and I would talk
and when fall started to chill
we bundled up.
She used to drink a lot of Tab
and that revved up a jittery,
sure-fire talk in her,
and I would try to calm her down.
Her skinny, wise-assed self
needed more buzz as much as
I needed more conversation.
When I left Syracuse without a word,
I sent her a case of Tab with a note that said
When I have gone, the sweetness comes.
But then I began to learn first hand
how life maims art. A few months later,
when I was alone and freezing in Madrid,
a friend sent me a note that said
Peggy cried. When I returned to school
I heard she had dropped out. We met once
a few years later almost by chance.
She said she was happily married.
There wasn't much more she could say.

Happy Endings

Happy trails and happy goodbyes
to once upon a time until we meet again
wild in the blue yonder. Happy those homes
whose treasures range where treasure maps say.
Happy the maps, and happy sweet dreams.
Happy the cottages from which the witches are fled
and happy the beds behind walls of stone
whose doors will withstand the wolf's ruff
huff and puff. Happy the queen whose magic
fits her slippers and happy the King
who brings her home. Happy the children
who bake their terrors away, the poor old
mother whose goose is golden
and uncooked, the boy who flees
and fells the monster he fears,
the thunder of his fall, the hole he fills.
Happy those who depend upon
the dependable thrum of bumble bees,
who lay themselves down under starry skies
and rock in the confidence of open arms.
Happy when they find themselves for ever
and ever protected when they rise.
Happy those under the tree on whom
the apple falls and the light turns on.
Happy those who fit the tune of poor cares
fled and plums thumbed. Happy Johnny
who scatters seeds and happy Jill at the still
and Jack with the crack in his crown
who drinks his fill and feels no pain
as he tumbles down. Happy those who
swing on porches with a view they love.
Happy the man in living colour and with
a big picture in his obit. Happy. Happy. All of it.

Retirement

Now
to unlearn
habits of
unhappiness
practised
since
way back when.

To lose them
one by one
until
what remains
is the other side
of then.

Tathagata

Stop reading this book
the book I'm reading says.
Walk away
from walking away
if you want to know
what can't be said.

I used to know ineffable.
I used to warm myself
at a wood-stove
outside Syracuse
and hear ineffable sing.
What did I know
about getting there
from anywhere?

Each night I read
a line at a time,
sometimes
the same line
again and again.

Morning

Came sun
came the raw call
of gull
came tug and fall
beached water
flopped
onto lichen
and stone

came deadheads
came bob and slip
of a hungry
subaqueous
pull
sheared tree
root side
up

came bay suck
light tied down
with yellow ropes

came the voice
of things.

Walking Around

We could go
whenever we like.
We could coffee up
and get lost in the random
maybe of streets we choose
by chance. We could train
from right-angled uptown
and get off the grid.

And when the beautiful
shop muses sing
we can choose to say
they are not beautiful
enough, and pass them by
as if they fulfilled
a less perfect desire.

We can pat ourselves
on the back for having
said no to the imperfect
hunger of our minds.

Last night's rain
freshened the streets
and as we walk
through puddles
and as they dry
our footsteps
can show us the way.

The Potter

The old hand
has thrown it on the wall
but the wall will not turn.
The hand has missed the wheel
and thrown it on the wall
that will not revolve.

So words upon the will
that will not turn.

Although engaged to the motions
of magnificent machines
that are always turning,
they do not turn as the earth turns
although while the earth turns
they are always turning.

Yoga, Sun Salutation:
Possible Clouds on the Way

for Madhur Anand

Just waking
when nothing
is clear
and anything
can come
between us
and the sun,
we do a routine
mindful
when we can.

Since we are
who we are
and it is
what it is
that's what
we do.

We take to the floor
and assume
postures
that warm us up
make us
more flexible
and strong.
We follow the leader,
do as she does.

And the pose
we consider benign
to neglect
we have to
stretch into
further than we can
if we want to get
to yes a lot.

That's it.
And not the sun,
since between us
any cloud can come.

What the Poem Is About

for Cornelius Eady

My brother died on the telephone
with a man who owed him
and would not pay.

They found his phone hanging
and him on the floor.

My father died in a rage
after bouncing a man
half his age.

I do not want
to go that way.

Any time of any day
I can fuse and die
as they did.

So this morning
I wrote this.

– Afterword –

A Drinkable Song

My parents used to sing their song
while sitting around the dining room.
They sang about sweet embraceable you,
and I don't care they sang.

When the beer appeared one afternoon
a case on a shoulder and a bill to pay,
Dad peeled a twenty right away
and bottoms up he crooned.

Dad liked it hot and Mom favoured cool.
They lived together by a lukewarm rule.
And when they sang they seemed to know
who they were and where to go.

I grew up singing with the morning light
sometimes bold and sometimes slight,
and when I sang I knew
what was what and who was who.

The beer is gone, their songs are sung,
but I still sing, and this was one.

ABOUT THE AUTHOR

Henry Rappaport received his B.A. with honours in English literature from Syracuse University, where he won the Whiffin Prize for poetry. At that time he studied with poets Donald Justice and Philip Booth along with the Henry Vaughn scholar, Robert Allen Durr. In particular, Durr's work on what he saw as the identity of the psychedelic and imaginative experiences was formative in the development of Rappaport's aesthetic. With a Danforth fellowship, Rappaport then went to the University of Washington where he studied with David Wagoner, receiving his M.A. for a collection of original poetry entitled *Spring Flowers This Year*.

In 1968 Rappaport immigrated to Canada and moved to Vancouver where he has lived ever since. He co-founded Intermedia Press, which published a variety of poetry and visual arts, producing such free media projects as Junk Mail and The Poem Company. Intermedia published his first four books of poetry: *Heat in the Heart*, *Are Words Things?*, *A Book of Days*, and *Dream Surgeon*. Over the years Intermedia Press morphed into a successful printing company in Vancouver, which Rappaport directed until its sale in 2003. Rappaport then brought his poetry to the fore, working with poets including Robert Hass, Don McKay and Karen Solie as well as in writers conferences at Sewanee, Bread Loaf, Sage Hill and others. Over the years he has been publishing in a number of North American journals, with his fifth book of poetry, *Loose to the World*, being the result of his poetic journey. Pre-publication comments refer to it as a book whose gyre-like structure supports a movement between poles of experience, including both the mystical and cynical in a simple plain-song style.

From time to time, Rappaport emails new poems to readers, who can subscribe at henryrappaport.com.